The 448th Bomb Group in No

Who were the 448th & why Norfolk?

The 448th Bombardment Group (H) was a part of the 20th Combat Wing, 2nd Air Division, which itself was part of the 8th Air Force, USAAF

During the turbulent days of World War II, Norfolk and the wider East Anglia became home to the Mighty Eighth Air Force as it took advantage of the relatively short flight time between the Norfolk coast and mainland Germany to get its war planes to Germany and back in the most advantageous manner. In the early part of this campaign, Seething Airfield became home to the 448th Bomb Group. Made up of the 712th, 713th, 714th and 715th Bombardment Squadrons, Station 146 as Seething was known to the American military, was the home to over 2,800 men who flew and maintained the 448th's B24 Liberators that operated on an almost daily basis to attack Airfields, Military and Industrial targets in Germany and Occupied Europe.

The 448th were activated at Gowan Field, Idaho, America and passed through Sioux City, Iowa; Herrington, Kansas and eventually Morrison Field, Florida for their final training and to prepare for their departure to Europe.

In late November, they arrived at Seething and took up residence in a base previously occupied by a small detachment of the RAF, who were there, working to get the base ready for the American's arrival. Only a few days later, on December 22nd, the 448th were fully operational, flying their first combat mission in support of the war effort. They had lost four aircraft en-route to the UK, so the reality of wartime flying was already starting to hit home.

This is how it looked to the men of the 448th, recorded on a day to day, basis by their own cameras.

Seething Aerodrome (Station 146) taken during the autumn of 1944.

The longest runway is North-East / South-West (07/25 - 2000yards) with the main technical site orientated to the centre right of the photo. The two cross runways were the traditional 1400 yards long and mainly used for landing only, when the wind was not suitable for the 07 / 25 runway. All runways were the standard 50 yard width.

Seething was just over nine miles to the south east of the city of Norwich, and close to the USAAF airfields of Hardwick and Flixton (Bungay). These three adjacent airfields formed the 20th Combat Wing. The small Suffolk market town of Bungay to the south was the nearest centre of urban life, as Seething was surrounded by a very rural environment, even for airfields traditionally located in fairly uninhabited farmland.

After hostilities ceased, the 448th went home and the RAF moved in for about ten years, moving out themselves in 1956. After a few years of neglect, the airfield became the home to the Waveney Flying Group and the Station 146 Tower Association.

Almost half the main runway, a section of the E/W secondary runway and some perimeter track still remain, as of course does the fully restored Control Tower.

Handover day. The RAF contingent depart (well, most of them anyway) and the 448th BG, USAAF take over.

Unlike many of the surrounding USAAF bases, when the RAF departed from Seething, they left behind a small handful of men.

The more 'formal' pose of one of these chaps, contrasts significantly with the less formal pose and attire of his American counterpart!

The 58th Station Complement Squadron arrived several weeks before the aircraft and their crews.

They spent their time getting the place sorted and to their liking…

…and having their photos taken.

Pretty soon the B24s started to arrive and it was down to work with a vengeance.

There were aircraft to prepare, maintenance to be done and of course, the missions to be flown. It was non-stop, round the clock. At Station 146, someone was always on the go. That's just how it was.

The aircrews headed off to find their garishly painted assembly ships, then turned south and east towards the enemy...

They all knew that the enemy were waiting for them…

…sometimes with devastating results.

Even large formations high above the cloud cover was not in itself protection from flak or the enemy fighters, you always kept a sharp look out…

…all too often, it wasn't enough.

…all too frequently for one or more of the crews it ended like this, in a field, somewhere in Europe.

Occasionally the damaged Liberator was kept flying by its crew and somehow coaxed back to England and its home base…

…many times it was just not possible.

Even if you got back to base, there were no guarantees that you could get your aircraft back down in showroom condition, or even in one piece.

With this amount of damage, luck played a big part in your arrival home.

They always said, 'any landing you can walk away from is a good one'.

Then I guess, on those terms, these were good ones…

…even if a bit adventurous as far as the aircrew were concerned.

Once in a while, walking away was never going to be an option…

While you might have missed the flak and the fighters on the mission, an 'interesting' landing like this could also claim its own tally of injured aircrew.

It kept the hospital team and the ground crews busy.

13

One team patched the crews up after a bad day…

…the other did the same for the aircraft.

The principle was the same. 'Keep them flying and get them back in the air as soon as possible'.

The B24s were maintained on the line, in the hangars and in individual specialist workshops.

The bikes they maintained where they stood. Wartime tyres and tubes were not the best quality.

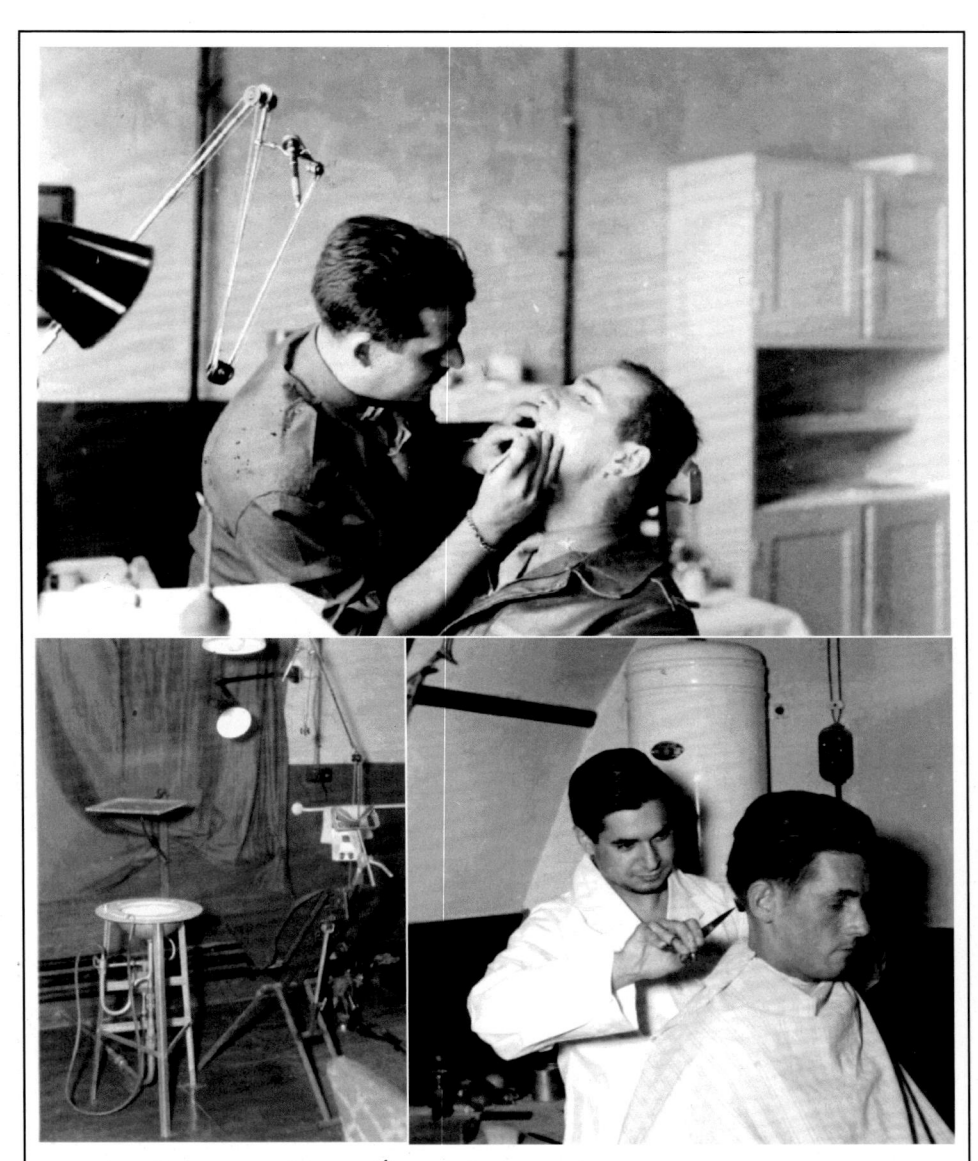

Occasionally the GIs of the 448th needed some maintenance too.
This was the station dentist at work. Somehow there doesn't look as much kit available to repair the GIs as there was for the B24s parked outside.
If you think the top photo makes the surgery look sparse, just take a look at the photo lower left, and see what it really was like!

Some said the station barber was better equipped!!! They may well have been right.

Once men and machines were declared fit for service, then the bomb dump, taxiway, runway and assembly ship, marked their route to Germany.

Here the co-pilot (Bart Lane) carries out some pre-flight checks. Sadly he and his crew were lost on the Magdeburg Mission, on 3rd Mar '45.

Bomb dump…
　　　Bomb trolley…
　　　　　Fuel bowser…
　　　　　　　…and off to work!

Another 448th B24 taxis out to join the queue heading to the main runway, at the start of another day's mission.

For some crews it would be their very first mission…

　　　…for others, it could well be their last.

As you climbed away from the airfield, you could not help but feel the guy that painted the Assembly Ship you were about to formate on...

...was also the guy painted the Air Traffic Control hut at the end of the runway - Using the same paint can!

Well at least it wasn't khaki!

The 448th…

…at work.

Berlin (Top) and The Seigfreid Line's 'Dragons Teeth' (Bottom), both familiar sights to the Bomber crews of the 448th.

They returned to Berlin many times in 1944/5.

The 'trolley' runs after the war had ended, gave the ground crews an opportunity to see what damage had been wrought.

A battered marshalling yard…

…or a POW camp…

…all somehow looked different on the battle maps and during the mission briefing back at base.

The destruction photographed by the 448th was the reality.

Destruction was not all one way. This is one of the 448th's B24s going down following an attack by Me262 jets, very close to the end of the war.

Inset photo of the crew just prior to the fateful mission. Only one crewmember survived, (2nd left top row); though that in itself must have been a miracle.

A year earlier, a much stronger enemy had followed the 448th home and attacked them as they landed back at Seething. Two crews and seven planes were lost.

On days like those, the Chaplins were some of the busiest guys on the station.

Left is the Protestant Padre on the right the Catholic Priest.

R&R was also a much needed respite after a bad day at the 448th. Here the joys of the Norfolk Broads are sampled by some of the crews…

…closer to home The Mermaid served a similar function, and allowed the 3 wheeled 'Pubmobile' to come into its own.

R&R also helped to take your mind off the hours you spent waiting around…waiting for things to happen…waiting for take off…waiting for the weather to clear…waiting for the squadrons to return from their missions.

On the other hand, if you were ground crew or part of the support team, it was a real nail-biting, stomach twisting wait to see if all the B24s you watched go out this morning, actually returned later in the day…

…all too often the numbers did not match.

For the Senior staff it was never an easy time…they were your boys.

Top Right   Col Gerry Mason

Top Left   Col Charles Westover

Bottom Right   Lt Col Hubert Judy

Bottom Left   Col James McK Thompson

The Senior Officers of the 448th Bomb Group in Europe.

29

The 'crud wagon' going down over Northern France.
Bombardier Charles Mc Bride (Inset right, on left of photo) evaded capture for 5 months before being liberated by a Canadian Tank squadron.
The photo was taken on that day!

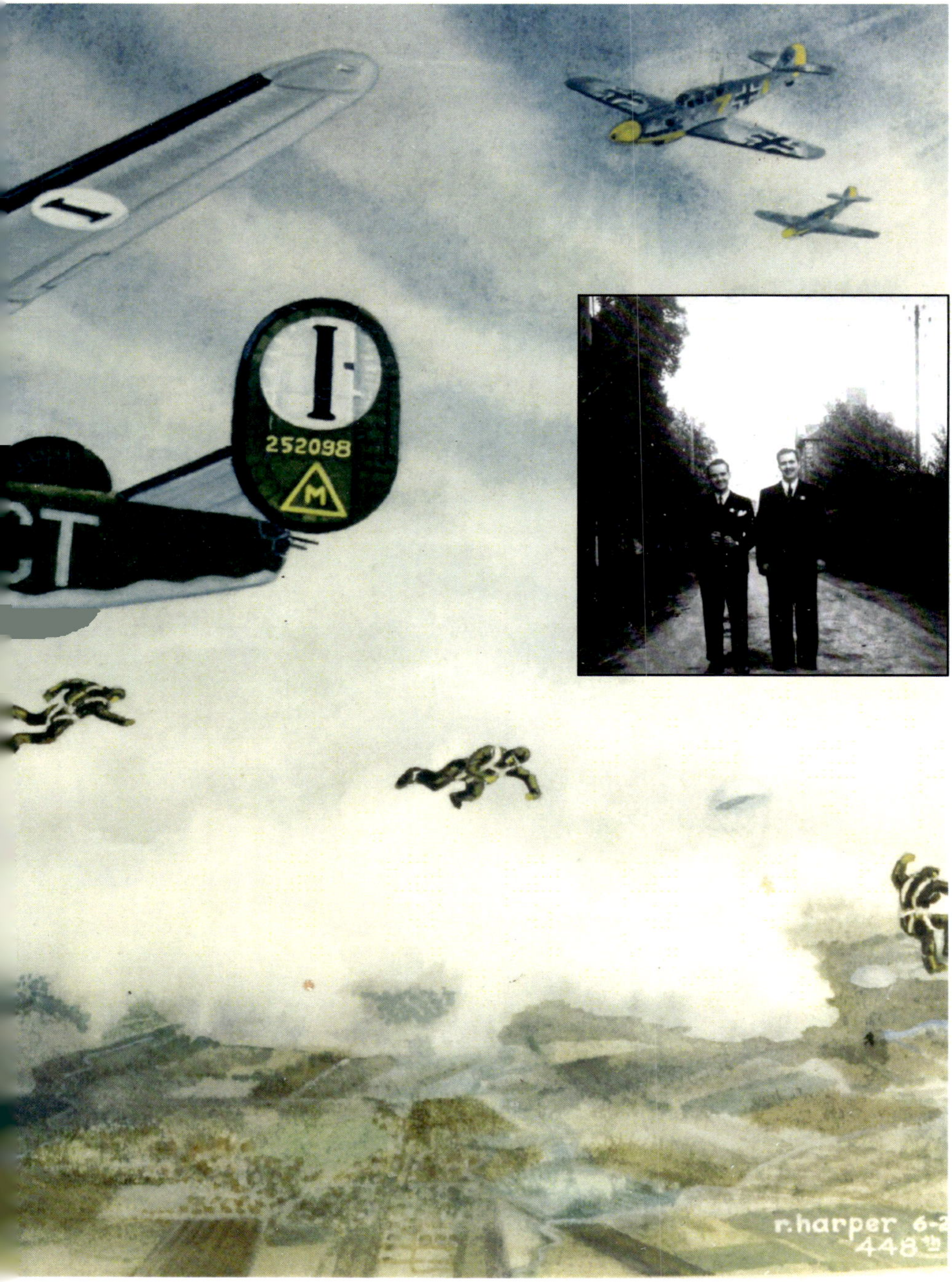
I
252098
M
CT
r.harper 6-2
448

The Bob Harper Murals.
All painted over, long before the war's end.

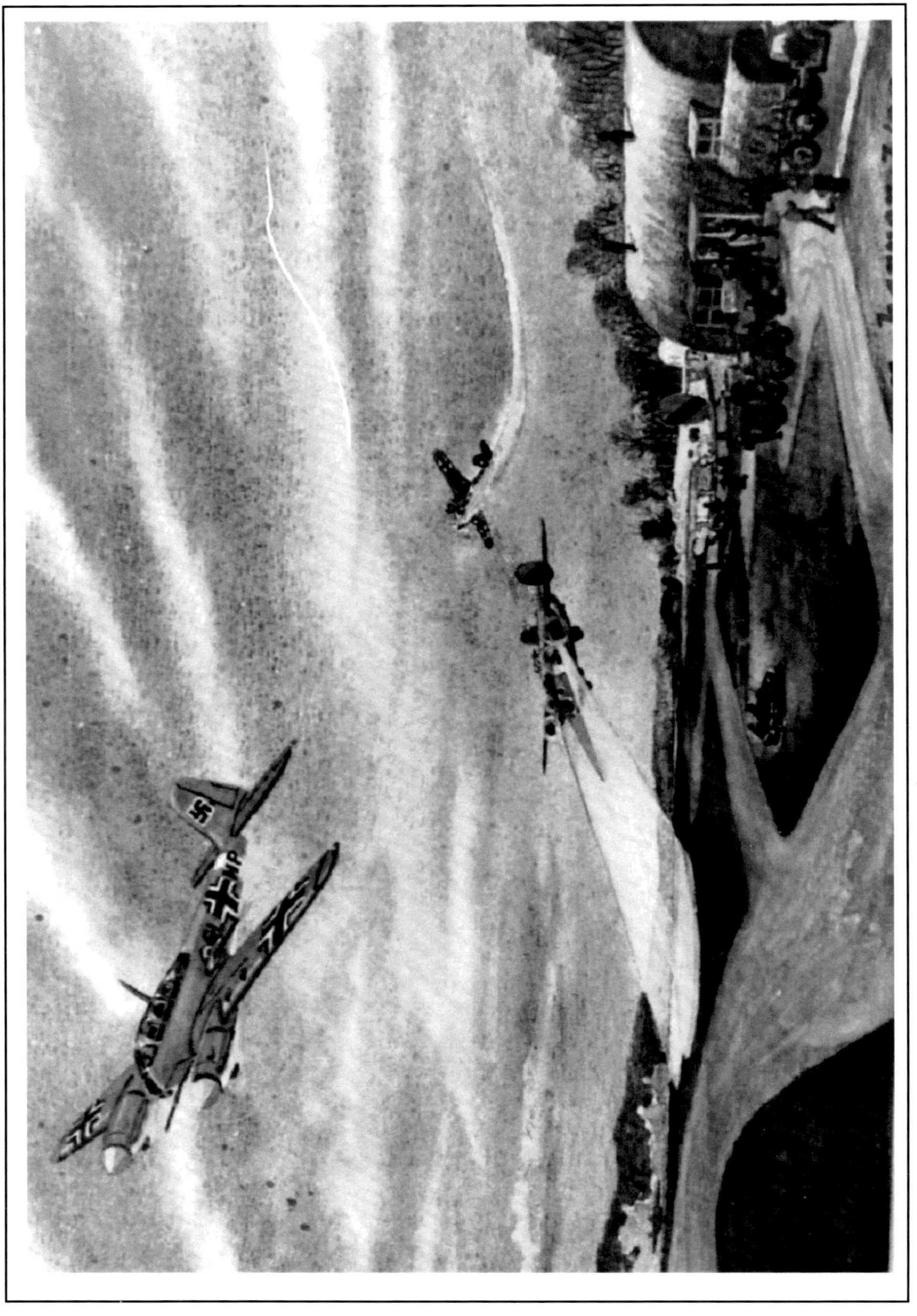

Bob Harper (left of fireplace), in real life an Assistant Intelligence Officer with the 448th Headquarters Detachment, stands with a colleague in front of one of his more imaginative murals that graced the mess.

Sadly the murals did not endear themselves to one of the station's COs who had them painted out long before the war's end.

Fortunately, a photographic record of most of them survived.

If the Mess was an important part of the 448th's 'social' life, then the Tower was of equal importance in its operational life. For a few brief hours every day, this place was the heart of the whole operation.

From the Seething Tower, looking to the North East.

Standing here, the runways were behind you.

Call-sign 'Bright Green', the Tower at Seething was home to what would nowadays be called Air Traffic Control, with both Approach and Ground radio calls being handled by the same controller.

For those returning planes with the radio, or the radio operator, out of commission, the light signals worked just fine.

From the Tower you could see across most of the whole airfield…

…This was the 714th Squadron site.

And these were the Maycrete huts which popped up just about everywhere across the site…

…and these were the huge T2 hangars on the Technical Site.

They were all part of the Station 146 skyline.

A shot from the water tower…this time the Nissen huts are the main feature.

This was the inside…it was home…and you were with your buddies.

At least the Norfolk winter allowed the snow to take the edge off the khaki for a week or two…

…and you could 'personalise' your hut with a snowman!

As if some aspects of the GI's life were not dangerous enough, someone suggested a slow bicycle race…on ice! (part of the 200th Mission celebrations). It had obviously seemed a good idea in the bar last night.

OK, so the snow did not help landings, or crash rescue.
Even 'visitors' ran out of luck sometimes.

Here a B24 from the 392nd BG gets wrecked close to the Seething Control Tower.
Low temperatures and icy runways were no help when you were in trouble…

…but then, some of the guys (aircrew) operated at temperatures of -40 every time they went on a mission…

…no one said it would be easy.

When you completed your mission quota, you got to go home. That was great…

…mind you, the first guy to achieve that, sure got the full treatment.

They put him in this outfit and paraded him around the base…

…with the CO's blessing!

The USAAF tradition of nose art was as strong at Seething as anywhere in the 8th Air Force.

Everyone had a photo taken by 'their' B24.

A lot of them were sent home to kid brothers and friends. Mom might have raised her eyebrows at some of them.

As with all 2nd Air Division Bomb Groups, the 448th's nose art came in all shapes and sizes.

Glamour and humour linked to memories of home were the traditional themes.

Frisco Frisky was impressive…not just the glamorous looks, but try counting the mission tally! There is ninety-six on the panel and there may still be some missing.

Daisy Mae and her very impressive tally of thirty seven missions completed…

…still not a patch on the Frisco Frisky.

This was the sort of shot you all sent home to the family, hoping that they wouldn't worry too much.

…And sometimes nose art was…well… just big.

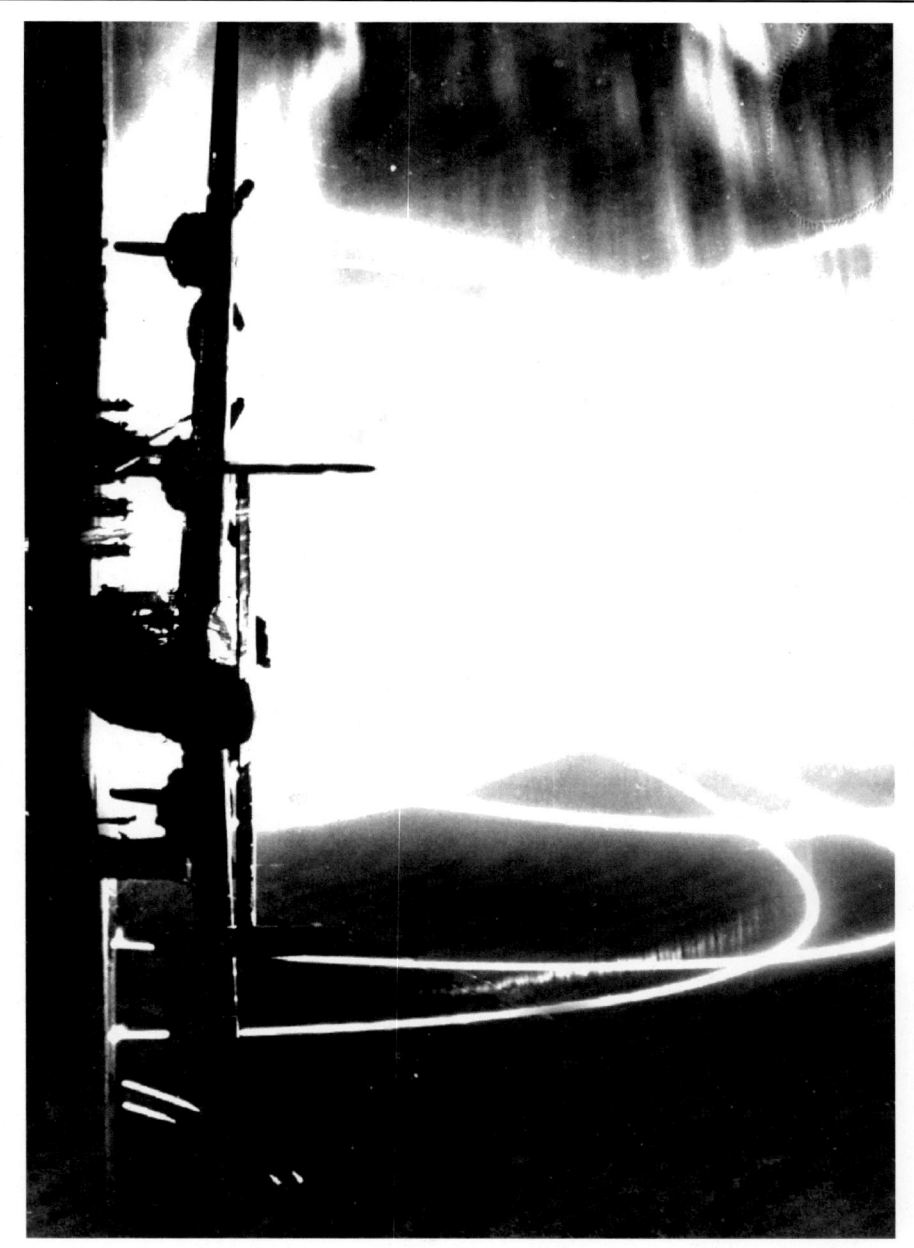

On VE Day, these pyrotechnics that lit up the Seething sky were very welcome…

…a few days ago they would have had a more sombre meaning.

As well as playing host to visiting entertainers from time to time, the 448th had its own resident band.

It also had a few 'home brewed' groups and trios.

They were all kept pretty busy.

It did not take long after their initial arrival for friendships to form. This young lad even stayed on camp, had his own bunk and helped out in the office, answered phones and generally made himself useful.

Even if the local children spoke a different English than the one you used in Kansas or Louisiana, they were still kids and they helped keep your feet on the ground.

After several years of war deprivations, candy bearing GIs were soon elevated up to hero status by most of the local youngsters.

The Christmas party for the local youngsters…

…and the dance at the Officers Club, all served to cement the friendships formed around the base.

"Why has he just put jam on my chicken?" A young Norfolk lad encounters thanksgiving Turkey and Cranberry Sauce for the first time.

No so many miles away, a USAAF officer gets his first quizzical view of a Yorkshire Pudding.

Friendship worked both ways, and USAAF personnel visited the homes of Norfolk villagers, living close by the base. Unsurprisingly it sometimes lead to more...

U.S. LANDING CARD
Necessary For Entry into the U.S.
Manifest No. 34
Line No. 14
U.S. Head Tax
U.S. Immigrant Inspector's Stamp

G.I. BRIDE

IDENTIFICATION TAG
WAR BRIDES
NAME VICHERY, SHEILA D.
DESTINATION Plymouth, Mass
TRAIN NUMBER / CAR NUMBER
WYNHAM
SPACE / TERMINAL FOR BAGGAGE

KEEP THIS CARD
SLEEPING QUARTERS

ROOM **B** 157

"QUEEN MARY"

I send you my best wishes for your happiness and good fortune in your new life in the great country of your adoption.

Love, romance and GI Brides…after the wedding came the bureaucracy. This is just some of the paperwork and labels needed to get the young brides back to their new homes.

This young bride was to travel on the Queen Mary in February 1946. From the end of the War, the Queen Mary had been criss-crossing the Atlantic regularly with returning American Personnel.

Some brides joined their new husbands in America after just a few weeks, others took over a year before they could make the journey and start their new life together.

Weddings ranged from grand events, to more modest family affairs…
…either way, it was a happy occasion that
lightened a dark period of many people's lives.

Station 146 Seething is blessed with several memorials to the men of the 448th. They are all well cared for and are worth a visit.

All photographs from or via the Patricia Everson 448th BG collection.
Cover painting by the late Harry Clow.
Centre painting by Bob Harper of the 448th HQ Detachment.

For further study, the authors recommend:-
               www.pastonroot.co.uk/golds/448.html
               The 448th Bomb Group(H) by Jeffrey Brett (Schiffer)

Facts and Figures on the 448th

Arrived   24th Nov 1943
Departed   6th July 1945

Aircraft Used   Consolidated Liberator B24
4 x 1,200 Pratt & Whitney Radial engines
10 man crew
Bomb load – 6 tons
All up weight – 29 tons
Top Speed – 290 MPH
Service Ceiling – 28,000 ft
Fuel Load – up to 3,516 gallons
Range – 2,100 miles

Bomb Group Complement
20th Combat Wing (H)
448th Bombardment Group (H) Headquarters
712th Bombardment Squadron (H)
713th Bombardment Squadron (H)
714th Bombardment Squadron (H)
715th Bombardment Squadron (H)
58th Station Complement Squadron
459th Sub Depot
1596th Ordnance Company
862nd Chemical Company
1193rd Military Police Company
2102nd Engineer Fire Fighting Platoon
1232nd Quartermaster Company
Det "B" 212 Finance Section
262nd Medical Dis RS (Avn)
18th Weather Station

Missions   *262 (7,343 Sorties)*

Ordnance dropped *15,286 Tons*

Losses 1943-1945 *Planes – 146*
                           Men – 498